HALLELUJAH

Sabrina Suarez

HALLELUJAH

Copyright © 2019 Sabiartistry, LLC, Sabrina Suarez.

All rights reserved. This book or any portion thereof may not be reproduced, stored in a retrieval system, or transmitted in any form or by any means including but not limited to electronic, mechanical, photocopy, recording, scanning, or any other form, except for brief quotations in critical reviews and articles or in social media sharing, without the prior written permission of the publisher.

Any references to historical events, real people, or real places are used fictitiously. Names, characters, and places are products of the author's imagination.

Printed by IngramSpark, in the United States of America.

ISBN: 978-1-7336332-0-8

Cover Design: Federico Paoli
Interior Design: Sabiartistry
Author photo: David Chuchuca

Sabiartistry LLC
www.sabiartistry.com

TABLE OF CONTENTS

Perspective

    1

Mental Illness

    12

I'm Sorry

    20

Repairs

    37

We're Doing the Best We Can

    50

Break the Cycle

    69

The World Deserves You

    78

About the Author

    97

As introductions go — I suck. Nothing feels authentic enough. So, we're going to jump right in. Just know, some of you might be triggered by this. It might push some buttons. Some buttons you didn't even know existed. It's important to remain open-minded, as I am just trying to show support to those supporters whose struggle goes undiagnosed. At times it may sound insensitive, but you get what you give, and if you go in with an open mind, you may be surprised by what you are gifted.

- perspective

Like the leaves blowing in the wind

separated from their kin

no one is undamaged

- decaying

What do you do
when what you want
is something they can't give to you?

- how long do I wait?

You were once my reprieve
but now you're just hurting me

The more I explain
the less traction I gain
in your head full of pain

My tears are traveling again
leaving familiar marks on my skin
they're begging you to let me in

I wish you'd listen to the sound of my voice when I say,
"You're enough"
you'd know I wasn't lying to you
not the way you do

Trust

It's such a delicate thing
and very rarely remains unbroken

I looked into the eyes of indifference
and found that pain is inevitable.

There comes a time where disappointment no longer describes how I feel,
there is just what was and what is

- my new reality

I promise you one day they'll realize they were never alone, and during moments of clarity, they'll see all that you have done for them, they'll take responsibility for their actions, they'll appreciate how much you have helped them — and all behind the scenes. Because not many other people get to see just how taxing it can be. But you've been there since the beginning and I understand how you'd want to see this through. I just hope, for your sake and mine too, that this clarity of mind comes before you show yourself the door and say, "I can't take this anymore."

- not a moment too soon

A JAILOR WITH NO BAILOR.

- MENTAL ILLNESS

We creep up and up and up
At a pace so agonizing
Until we reach the top

It's bliss

Just when I start to think
'It can't get any better than this'

Not a question
But a statement

We fall into an abyss
It's the deepest dark there is

My stomach flies into my chest
I feel hopeless

Panicked

And then I think 'I'll never see the light of day again'

That is, until we begin to ascend

Again

- I've never really liked rollercoasters

It's not always easy being your number one fan. In fact, I get frustrated just like anybody else can and I feel I must keep it to myself for the sake of your mental health. I don't know when I should be tough or when I should be courteous, when you haven't gotten up in days and it's not looking like that will change. They say there is a line between empathy and enabling. That is a line I have still yet to see. Maybe it's drawn in the sand?

The same sand that slips from the top of the hourglass to the bottom. We call this rock bottom. It's a place I hope we don't stay.
Here, we are stagnant.

- the wait

You say you're scared to tell everyone what you're going through. And while they make assumptions about what's really happening, placing blame on the people who are just trying to help you stay sane in an effort to explain what is going on to themselves, you sit and wait, hoping it will all just go away, and you'll never have to face the discomfort a conversation that serious can create. While you do this, I'm the one they place blame on. I understand they're just looking for answers, but they're not asking the right questions — or any questions for that matter. Don't worry though, I'll continue to smile, tight-lipped and flattered, so you don't have to communicate *just how* painful your mind has made your life. And after, we'll reminisce on all the suffering we did.

- I'm just happy you're alive

I was told the term *triggered* meant to set off a chain of events
what it really meant
was screaming at the top of your lungs
so that the rage and the hate that runs through your veins can finally have a name
gripping the closest thing to you and inhaling so sharply you'd think you pierced a lung, allowing blood, that runs thick with fear and blame, to fill your rib cage
what it meant was
losing control of your brain and reacting in a way you wouldn't be proud of tomorrow, but today,
is ok

triggered is knowing you're losing the people you care for the most and not being able to do a damn thing to keep them as safe as you'd hoped
that's triggered

Your spirit ebbs and flows

with the tide

when it recedes

it leaves

nothing in its wake

We've joked about you leaving

like we've joked about my singing
like we've joked about our upbringing

I'm always joking, trying to bring some light to your darkest places
it doesn't work, really

I don't know if it ever did

You can try to hide
but the day will break
and you will see
I just hope it's not too late

I'M SORRY.

It hurts to think of a world without you in it
but when I tell you
it doesn't seem to make a difference

I begged and begged
"Try"
you said, "I will," but never did

you weren't ready yet
you hadn't chosen yet

- to live

You can't take responsibility for everything
they must want it for themselves

you can offer support
but if they don't want to hear you out

don't

- don't kill yourself

I hope you choose to stay
if not, that's ok
I understand
but I'll never get used to introducing you by saying, "I once
knew a man..."

I didn't realize then I was looking into the eyes of a man who had already decided he was dead.

"It's easier"

the most complicated words I have ever heard

Do you ever feel like you witnessed a murder?

- you thought pain was temporary, but it pulled the trigger

Losing someone is excruciating. You're wounded, physically and emotionally. Left with a nasty scar, constantly reminding you of your grief, and at a moment's notice that wound could open back up. Reacquainting you with an aching only you recognize. When it does, you welcome the heartbreak back as if you're old friends, praying you'll never have to see them again.

I'll accept grief

if it means I had the opportunity

to feel

for connection doesn't come cheap

My heart hurts
with the tears shed
I bleed clear
it's the emptiness

My injuries weren't self-inflicted like yours were
but they could be traced
like yours
back to the same source

Life saver
by nature
all I hear is
save her

- s.o.s

I asked you what was keeping you here
and you couldn't tell me a single thing

except it might not work and you were right

it wasn't going to work

I wasn't going to let it

- enough is enough

I signed

on the dotted line

vowing to keep you safe

knowing it may not mean forever

but that we will take what resembles it

You were fighting a war only you could win

you were waging a battle

that consumed everything

including your soul

just when I thought you were going to give in

you raised your white flag

signaling your undeniable victory

- hallelujah

You told "the end"
it would have to wait

HE HAD AN 'OUT OF ORDER' SIGN PERMANENTLY CHAINED AROUND HIS NECK.

- REPAIRS

I thank fate every day for allowing you to stay.

"I'm not done here,"

said with enough resolve

could mean the world to someone who's already given up

"I'm ok"

was the best thing I had heard in a long time

Your "I'm ok"
is my "Let's celebrate!"

Hope —

I pick you up and dust you off

as good as new

but not

- you let me down

How do I know it's real
when all I've ever known
was a false sense of security
disguised as happy?

- a mirage

Relief is not routine to me

I'm more familiar with worry

The scariest part was that I grew used to savoring every memory, thinking one day there wouldn't be any.

Coping skills

- our new thrills

I know what hard is
I've lived it

what I don't know
is what hard isn't

Your smile

kills

and heals

me

- all at the same time

You thanked me tonight
for keeping you alive
for helping you survive
but it's me who will never be able to repay you
for saving me the 'goodbye'

WE'RE DOING THE BEST WE CAN.

I am a tree whose bark has been marred by the names of the aggrieved.

- permanency

Just when we thought there was only an up

you taught us it is immediately followed by a down

You are my soul to keep
so keep
going

You're determined to push me away

congratulations

today is that day

You try to justify your actions
all the attitude and misplaced anger
but you can't decide for me
how I feel about anything

especially you

You read about your worth, but never took my word for it.

I'm coming to the realization I won't always be there to put your pieces back together.

Today's a bad day
I wish I could say
I'll still be here to see the good

You were the birthplace of boundaries
and I am a country
whose borders have been tested mercilessly
and though I have every right to be guarded
I'm still accepting refugees

I've become lost in your sea
I'm forgetting how to breathe

"I'm sorry things didn't work out between us," he confesses. The crack that echoes through my chest is comparable only to that of an ax, whose sharpened edge repeatedly pierces the shell of a log in opposition. I am left exposed and offering the only truth I know. One that will never do him justice.

"Don't be. You were never a mistake to me."

Devoted

Appreciated

Resilient

Kind

- all you are

You see a facade
I see evidence that you're wrong
hoping that you'll see you're strong

You are my anchor —
steady, yet always descending

I heard you laugh for the first time in a while. It was the genuine kind — my favorite kind. The type of laugh that bounces off every wall. The type of laugh that I can hear on repeat for days. The type of laugh that hurts. It hurts your stomach because you can't stop. It hurts my heart because it's all I've wanted to hear and can't anymore.

My bright light
in a dark night
my Chester Bennington
thirty-six hours before he died

You matter.
You matter.
You matter.

So much of me depends on if you're happy.

I will not rest until you and happiness have met

- you deserve each other

BREAK THE CYCLE.

Imagine being on an airplane
you're soaring through the air without a care
in the world, when suddenly,
you're told
to brace for a crash landing
and soaring becomes hanging
on for dear life
and you look to your friend, your partner, your child, your
reason to be alive
and have to decide
to put your mask on first
or you both die

it's that hard

- self-care

Note to self:

Let it go

- guilt

Relinquishing any control I thought I had

- forgiveness

All the things I was looking for you to give me, I started giving myself

- thank you

I've found me without you

- we made it

For once, alone doesn't feel so lonely

as far as company, I am content with my own

I am marked

discolored by the lives of others

my hue unmistakably altered

made complex, vibrant, and rich

distinctly vivid

- a work of art

Don't do as you're told
don't get dragged into the mess that is their mold
skewed, broken, deformed —
instead show them beautiful
show them reform

- be their muse

THE WORLD DESERVES YOU.

Seek help *for yourself* before anyone else.

Recovery requires a lot of maintenance

and patience

a lack of patience creates patients

Take pride —

your progress has not been painless

yet here you are

Your worth is not negotiable.

You are perfect.

You are worth it.

The only two truths you need to believe.

Who you should be

Who you could be

Who you are

- decisions

Your potential is endless.

It's a disease, not a disguise.

- you're still *people* in my eyes

Let's make conversations about mental illness
about strength
not weakness

Set stigma adrift

and wade through the unworthy with grace

Like the depths of the ocean we have yet to explore

there is so much more to you than is known

Be gentle with yourself
not because you're fragile
that was never the case
it's because of your strength
you've earned it

"It will get easier" is a myth
those people live in an ignorant bliss
it will be a fight full of fists, teeth, and grit
but you're strong
you will defeat it

Confident

Light

Independent

Motivated

Brave

- all you will become

When you reach the happy ending of your story

you'll be grateful you flipped the page

A caterpillar's transformation into a butterfly is grueling. It must change from one form to another by first becoming nothing. Do you think this would be possible if it weren't capable of withstanding such a feat? Do you think it questions its own capabilities? Do you appreciate the beauty of the butterfly, knowing this is how it came to be?

- it wouldn't be beauty without the struggle

I tell the story — really tell the story — from start to finish. As I'm going, I don't think too much about it, reciting details in such an uninterested way one knows they have become commonplace. That I've reviewed them. And it would seem I've come to terms with all that they mean.

In reality, I've just been waiting for someone to show an interest in hearing the whole thing. It wasn't until I'd shared my inner grief that I realized I could find the freedom we all so desperately seek.

This was my journey to peace.

To supporters:
Take care of yourself.
To my inspiration:
Please, don't give up.
Hallelujah.

ABOUT THE AUTHOR

Sabrina Suarez is an ambitious and passionate advocate, motivator, inspiration-seeker, soul-searcher, goal-chaser, and overall creative. She is a writer, life and confidence coach, social worker, volunteer, and graduate student.

She has dedicated her life to being of service to others. She formed her own business, Sabiaristry, where she offers life and confidence coaching services that assist others in developing strategies that allow them to create positive change in their lives, at the young age of twenty-three.

Sabrina currently resides in Massachusetts with her pitbull-mix, Red. Learn more about Sabrina by visiting www.sabiartistry.com. Any and all business inquires can be made via the website or via email: sabiartistry@gmail.com.

Sabrina can also be found on social media:

@SABIARTISTRY & @BOOKSBYSABI

www.ingramcontent.com/pod-product-compliance
Lightning Source LLC
Chambersburg PA
CBHW071217070526
44584CB00019B/3061